I remember what a blessing Goodwin's *The Return of* ago. So I'm delighted to se accessible version. It's a bool pastoral wisdom, but even better it is full of warm-hearted gospel exhortations to treasure our relationship with God in Christ.

Tim Chester
Faculty member of Crosslands Training
and pastor of Grace Church, Boroughbridge

With clear prose set within coherent outline form, this classic treatment of prayer helps us explore one of the great mysteries and blessings of biblical faith. In what ways do the expressed desires of God's people, disciplined in mind and heart by the word of God, have an effectual influence on the God 'who works all things after the counsel of his own will'? Paul expressed confidence to the Corinthians that God would deliver him: 'you also helping together in prayer for us' (2 Cor. 1:11). Goodwin, distilled to essence by these gifted editors, opens to the reader the theology of prayer offering explanation, encouragement, admonition, warning, and assurance. One impressive aspect of this short book is its witness to how much of the Bible actually is written in the context of prayer. Though the 'return of prayers' is mysterious, it is no esoteric activity but at the heart of biblical revelation and the providential operations of God. This book is a sentence by sentence reminder of that great grace.

Tom J. Nettles
Senior Professor of Historical Theology, The Southern
Baptist Theological Seminary, Louisville, Kentucky

There is much written on the subject of prayer, but very little on answers to prayer. There is pastoral wisdom in this little book, and it is good to see it in simplified form.

Bill James
Principal, London Seminary, London

GRACE
ESSENTIALS

THE RETURN
OF PRAYERS

THOMAS GOODWIN
PREPARED BY DAVID HARMAN

CHRISTIAN
HERITAGE

Copyright © Grace Publications Trust 2021

paperback ISBN 978-1-5271-0613-0
epub ISBN 978-1-5271-0689-5
mobi ISBN 978-1-5271-0690-1

First Published in 1997
This revised edition published in 2021
in the
Christian Heritage Imprint
by
Christian Focus Publications Ltd,
Geanies House, Fearn, Ross-shire,
IV20 1TW, Scotland, U.K.
www.christianfocus.com
and
Grace Publications Trust
7 Arlington Way
London, EC1R 1XA, England.
www.gracepublications.co.uk

Cover design by Pete Barnsley
Printed by Bell & Bain, Glasgow.

Contents

Part Two: God speaking peace

Part Three: The folly of turning back

Editor's Introduction

Thomas Goodwin (1600-1680), a Congregationalist, was one of Oliver Cromwell's top advisers and served under his appointment as president of Magdalen College, Oxford. Before his conversion he was ambitious and sought popularity but afterwards made it his aim to speak as simply as possible. His contemporaries recognised his great ability in explaining and applying the Scriptures and they also respected him as a man who had no ambitions for himself but only wanted to do the best in whatever he was called to do.

In *The Return of Prayers* Goodwin is at his best, expounding with clarity and insight the words of Psalm 85:8: 'Let me hear what God the Lord will speak, for he will speak peace to his people, his saints; but let them not turn back to folly'. Psalm 85 prophesies the return of the Jews from Babylonian captivity. It is also a prayer that God's people might once again enjoy their former blessings. The psalmist urges the Lord to be gracious to His church, recalling to mind former deliverances. Then, having finished his prayer, he awaits an answer from heaven. 'Let me hear what God will say', he says. And then, having gained an answer of peace, he uses that blessing as a spur to perseverance.

Goodwin's original work is in three sections. These are retained here along with Goodwin's original chapter divisions. The first section, Listening to what God has to say, is the largest and contains the central message that Goodwin wished to emphasise. He writes to help Christians become more convinced of the value of prayer and to persevere in it. Some Christians give up praying because they feel that God is not answering their prayers. Others are perplexed by God's answering them in a different way from what they expect. Some believers do not take the trouble to observe God's answers and thereby lose comfort and blessing. The simplification of this section presented here was prepared by David Harman and was originally published as part of a book on prayer, entitled 'What happens when I pray?' (Grace Publications, 1997).

The author's introduction and the remaining two sections complete Goodwin's original work and are presented here for the first time. They were prepared by Andrew Shrimpton and Mike Adams. The second section, God speaking peace, brings assurance that God will answer and bring His peace, even if it does not always fit our timetable. In the third section, The folly of turning back, Goodwin is full of pastoral concern. He warns about the foolishness of turning away from God after He has answered our prayers for forgiveness, he shows that assurance of peace should motivate us to holiness, and he encourages those that stumble with the wonderful mercy of God; but he warns us never to take these things for granted. Peace has been bought for us at a great price and must never be lightly esteemed.

Author's Introduction[1]

God has infinitely great riches for us in Christ. He has given the Holy Spirit to help us know what these riches are and to provide access to them. The Spirit intercedes for us when we do not know how to pray.

Through the great privilege of prayer we share in Christ's work as prophet, priest and king. As priests, we offer up our prayers as spiritual sacrifices, acceptable to God through Christ. As kings, we rule with God. We become, as it were, part of His council. He listens to the petitions we make. As prophets, we speak in our prayers of things to come, which God brings into being through our prayers. God's ways are beyond our understanding, but if we delight in His Word, we will be able to pray intelligently and we can, to some extent, prayerfully and intelligently participate in what He is doing.

God uses us and our prayers as a king uses his servants to carry out his purposes. It is a great honour to be co-workers with God in this way. We should try to understand what God is doing and delight in His ways. 'Great are the works of the LORD, studied by all who delight in them' (Ps. 111:2). Surely

---

1. Originally a letter addressed to Sir Nathaniel Rich.

we should particularly study God's mercies given to us in answer to our prayers. We can see them as personal messages of love written in His own hand.

We can take particular delight in the wonderful ways in which God is willing to bless us personally. His promises are like pre-printed forms with blank spaces in which we can fill in our names and return the forms to God in prayer. When we have stretched our desires as far as possible, God is still able to do far more than we can ask or even imagine (Eph. 3:20).

Time spent praying and claiming God's promises would be greatly enriching to us. It is the praying Christian who makes use of the riches of God's promises, like a wise and diligent merchant seeking to bring in glory to God, good to the church, and grace and comfort to his own soul. And how infinitely rich must that man become who trades with God's riches!

We should then put effort into studying how God is answering our prayers. We shall miss out if we only pray earnestly but don't look out for the answers. A merchant must not only be diligent in trading but also keep careful records of the returns on his investments.

Some people do not realise that this is their duty. They are careful to pray, but they do not expect a return on their prayers until the final judgment. Others receive speedy answers to prayer; but because God does not answer exactly as they expect, they fail to realise that He has answered them and so they disregard His answers. Many people, when the answers to their prayers are long delayed, become discouraged and give up—like a merchant who assumes that his ships have sunk because they are delayed at sea and he has no news of them.[2]

---

2. Goodwin was writing, of course, long before the days of instant communication by radio, telephone and the internet.

We are too ready to complain that little comes of our praying. We shall lose our encouragement and God will be robbed of His rightful praise if we don't keep a careful reckoning of answers to our prayers.

This little book is written to encourage believers in this important duty and to point out things that may discourage us from it. I should particularly like to help young and weak believers to understand the relationship between their prayers and what God is doing in His answers.

Dedicated, in gratitude to God, to the memory of
Miss Stephanie Wright
(former Librarian of the Evangelical Library)
who first proposed an abridgement of
The Return of Prayers
and began the work before her sudden death in a
tragic road accident in 1990.

Part One

Listening to what God has to say

'Let me hear what God the LORD will speak …'

Prepared by David Harman

1

God's people are to take careful note of the answers to their prayers

Firstly, when we have prayed to God we can be sure that He will answer us. 'My God will hear me', says the prophet Micah (Micah 7:7). 'I will … look out to see what he will say to me', says Habakkuk (2:1). Why should we do this? Because we shall despise God's gracious provision for us if we think that prayer will not be any use in bringing about the purpose for which God has ordained it. Every faithful prayer is ordained by God to be a means of obtaining what we desire and pray for. 'This is the confidence that we have towards him [God], that if we ask anything according to his will he hears us' (1 John 5:14). It is true that God hears an enemy, but this is not the kind of meaning we are talking about. God hears His people's prayers with favour. God's ears are said to be open to their prayers, and so John follows his statement by saying in the next verse, 'And if we know he hears us in whatever we ask, we know that we have the requests that we have asked of him' (1 John 5:15). Our prayers are granted as soon as we have prayed, even though the process of fulfilling our requests has not yet begun. As soon as a godly man prays, the prayer instantaneously arrives in heaven and the petition is immediately granted. As soon as Daniel prayed, an answer was given, although the angel that brought that message did not arrive until some time later (Dan. 9:20-23). No prayer is ever useless. Where God has given a heart to speak, He has an ear to hear. To think otherwise is to despise God's gracious provision for us.

Secondly, if we are not confident that our prayer is going to be heard, we are not only misusing God's provision for us. We are also misusing His name. You evidently think God's arm is too short to save or His ear too dull to hear. You thus rob God of one of His most royal titles, for He describes himself as 'a God that hears prayer'. You should remember that the petitions of God's people do not pass out of His sight until He sends an answer. After David had prayed, he said that he waited for an answer more than watchmen wait for the morning (Ps. 130:6). Elsewhere David says, 'O Lord, in the morning you hear my voice; in the morning I direct my prayer to you and watch' (Ps. 5:3, margin). He expected an answer.

Thirdly, if God gives you an answer and you take no notice of it, you let God speak to you in vain. That is a great insult to God. Our speaking to God in prayer and His answering us form a great part of our experience of walking with God. We should study His dealings with us and compare our prayers with His answers. In 1 Kings 8:56 Solomon states that not one word had failed of all God's good promises. We should regard our prayers as a way of putting God's promises into action.

Again, if you do not wait for the Lord to speak, you will provoke Him not to answer you at all. God will see that it will be quite useless for Him to answer. It is not enough just to pray. After you have prayed, you need to listen for an answer, so that you may receive what you have prayed for. Otherwise, you will not observe God fulfilling your prayers. How then will you bless God and give Him thanks for hearing you?

Watchfulness and thankfulness are required in prayer (Col. 4:2). Perhaps the reason you pray so much and give thanks so little is because you take such little notice of God's answers. When we have offered a faithful prayer, God is made our debtor because of His promises. We are to take note of His payment and give Him a receipt. Otherwise, God loses some of the praise due to Him. And if God is the loser so you will be too. You will lose the experience you might have had through it—an experience of God and His faithfulness. If you have proved God again and again in answering your prayers, such experiences will give you hope and confidence in God at other times. David says, 'Because he inclined his ear to me, therefore I will call on him as long as I live' (Ps. 116:2). It is as if he had said, 'Now that God has heard me, I know where to go. This experience, even if I had no more, is enough to encourage me to go on praying to God'.

Furthermore, by observing God's answers to your prayers, you will gain an insight into your own heart, ways and prayers, and learn how to judge them. David's assurance that he did not have sinful desires in his heart was strengthened by God's having heard his prayers. He reasons like this: 'If I had cherished iniquity in my heart, the Lord would not have listened. But truly God has listened; he has attended to the voice of my prayer' (Ps. 66:18-19). If God does not answer your petitions, it will make you enquire as to the reason for it. You will then examine your prayers and the state of your heart to see

17

whether, in fact, you had prayed with wrong motives (see James 4:3). If you have a friend who is usually punctual in answering your letters but who then fails to answer you in a particular matter, you begin to think that something must be wrong. You then take steps to find out what has caused the delay. Perhaps you have offended your friend in some way. It is like this with your prayers. If you do not take careful note of answers to prayer you will lose much comfort. There is no greater joy than seeing prayers answered. 'Ask, and you will receive, that your joy may be full', says Jesus (John 16:24). As it is a great joy to see anyone converted, it is an even greater joy to the one who has been the means of it. To see God do much good to His Church, and hear others' prayers for it, is a comfort. How much more is it a joy to see God do it as a result of one's own prayers! That God and we should be of one mind and desire the same things is a cause for great joy. It is wonderful when we see that we ourselves have been answered. You lose much comfort and blessing when you do not take note of the answers to your prayers.

2

How to find out God's intentions
towards you when you pray

How do you recognize answers to your prayers and how do you know when God is taking action in response to them?

You must be content to see some prayers never answered in your own lifetime. For example, the fulfilment of your prayers for the utter downfall of God's enemies and the flourishing of the gospel must wait for the Church to reap in years to come. Such prayers will not be lost. If they are offered up by the eternal Spirit they have eternal significance. For instance, the prayer that Stephen made for his persecutors (Acts 7:60) was fulfilled after his death in the conversion of Saul of Tarsus. David's prayer against his enemy in Psalm 109:8-9 had its final fulfilment about a thousand years later in the downfall of Judas (Acts 1:20). When the prophets predicted the sufferings of Christ and the glories that would follow, it was revealed to them that they were not serving themselves, but us (1 Pet. 1:10-12). So in prayer, if we pray with the guidance of the Holy Spirit, we may ask for many things that will come to pass much later. Perhaps God will reveal to you by a secret impression on your spirit that He will use your prayers, among others, for the accomplishment of His purposes in days to come. In this way, God gives you an assurance that He has accepted you as belonging to Him.

God never revealed His love more to Moses than when he prayed for God's people. One of the best evidences of the uprightness of your heart is that you can pray for the good of the Church for a long time to come, even though you may never see it with your own eyes. When you reach heaven, your joy will be full when you see that your prayers have resulted in the conversion of those for whom you prayed, and the ruin of the Church's enemies. There is joy in heaven over one sinner who repents. Similarly, those whose prayers are used by God in any matter will have great reason to rejoice in heaven!

3

How God answers prayer for our relatives, friends and physical blessings

We are commanded to pray for others. See, for example, James 5:16 and 1 John 5:16. How are such prayers answered? We know that such prayers are often granted. Why else would God make promises concerning them? God gives us promises to encourage us to pray and to witness His abundant love for us. It is a sign that we are in extraordinary favour with God when He hears us, and an evidence of our priesthood. We have this favour through the fellowship we have with Christ as our High Priest. God has made us kings and priests to prevail and intercede for others. If God hears prayers for others, how much more will He hear us for our own needs? When Christ healed the paralytic (Matt. 9:2) it is recorded that He took note of the faith of those who brought the man to Him. This Scripture is intended to encourage us to bring others to the Lord in prayer.

Our prayers for others, however, may often not be answered in the way we hoped. Samuel's prayer for Saul was not granted (compare 1 Samuel 15:11 with verse 35). Prayer is like other means that God has instituted for the good of others. We may preach to many and yet few may believe. Similarly, we may pray for many, not knowing who are appointed to receive eternal life. However, although we do not know what will happen, we are still to pray for them (1 Tim. 2:1-4). Where God gives opportunity for preaching it is more than likely that He has some people to convert. Usually the Word of God takes root among some, though often in only a few.

In the same way, when God has stirred up our hearts to pray for others it is a sign that He will hear us for at least some of them. God may, in His wisdom, deny our requests for some. God requires us to pray out of duty, because prayer is a means ordained by Him through which He often brings things to pass. However, God has not bound Himself to answer every prayer in exactly the same way as we have asked. There is certainly a universal and general promise that God will hear and accept prayer, but He does not promise always to grant the specific thing prayed for. God makes similar promises concerning other means of doing men good, such as our reproofs or our preaching. For example, the promise of healing in James 5:15 cannot be universal. If the promise were universal, we might conclude that sick men for whom prayer had been made would never die. But we know it is appointed for all men to die. This Scripture in James is a provision to which God has attached a gracious promise, because He often does restore the sick through prayer, although not in every case. On any particular occasion, we must rely upon God to fulfil His promises, quietly resting upon His Word. We cannot, however, have a full assurance that we shall obtain everything we ask for, because the promise is not universal, but indefinite.

This can be illustrated by reference to other promises of a temporal or outward nature. There is a promise of long life to those who honour their parents, yet we know from experience and from the Scripture that it does not always turn out that way. This particular promise, therefore, cannot be absolute, infallible or universal, but only indefinite.

While we must approach such promises in faith, we must do so quietly resting in God and in submission to His will. We must submit to God's good pleasure as to the way He disposes of the matter. Faith must embrace the promises in general in full belief that God means what He has said, and that He certainly will fulfil His promises according to His purpose. However, we must not assume that in any particular instance God's promises will be fulfilled to us in exactly the same way as we have asked. The truth, purpose and intent of the promise is not universal, but indefinite. God does not require of us an absolutely full persuasion that He will perform a promise to us in any particular manner. God requires only an act of dependence, quietly resting in His will. Nevertheless, if God should at any time give us a special faith concerning any particular temporal blessing for ourselves or others, we may be certain that we shall receive it.

When God gave the apostles power to work miracles, they were bound to believe that the miracles would without fail be performed by them, as in the case of casting out demons. Thus Jesus on one occasion rebukes them for lack of faith in this respect (Matt. 17:19-20). It is in this way that Jesus' words in Matthew 21:21-22 are to be understood: 'If you have faith and do not doubt … even if you say to this mountain, "Be taken up and thrown into the sea", it will happen. And whatever you ask in prayer, you will receive if you have faith.' When God works in us such a faith we must believe with absolute certainty that the thing will be done, and it shall be done. But God does not always call us to such a kind of special faith. If God did stir up such a faith, He would accomplish the thing asked for but, in general, promises made about outward things are not universal, but indefinite. We cannot, therefore, believe with absolute certainty that God is under obligation to bestow any temporal blessing on ourselves or others in response to our prayers.

When we pray for others and yet God does not see fit to grant that particular blessing, then although our prayers seem to be returned to us unanswered, they will return for our good. In Psalm 35:12-13, David said that he prayed for his enemies when they were sick but that his prayers were returned to him unanswered. In his prayers, David showed the sincerity of his heart towards God and his true forgiveness of his enemies. Although his prayer did not profit his enemies, it turned to David's own good. It came back with blessings for himself. God stirs up in His children this willingness to pray for their enemies, but He does not always mean to answer those prayers in the way that has been asked. He means to draw forth and reward those holy attitudes of heart which are the noblest part of God's image in His children and with which He is so much delighted.

If we have prayed for a long time for those whom God does not intend to bless, He will in the end remove our desire to pray for them. What God did by a revelation from heaven to Samuel (1 Sam. 16:1) and to Jeremiah (Jer. 7:16), He does now by a less obvious method. He will withdraw the Holy Spirit's assistance in prayer. God does this because He is loath not to hear His people when they pray. When God does not mean to hear, He lays the key of prayer out of the way, so desirous is He to give answers to every prayer.

Sometimes God will let us pray for the conversion or good of someone He does not intend to bless. He does this to show that His thoughts are not the same as ours, for He may then answer those prayers in the life of some other person. This will give us as much joy as if He had answered us according to our original intent. Abraham prayed for Ishmael, but God gave him Isaac instead (Gen. 17:18-19). You may perhaps pray for one person more than another out of natural affection. God, however, may answer you by blessing another for whom, perhaps, your heart was not so much stirred. When the latter is converted, it proves to be as great a comfort as if the former for whom you had prayed had been blessed.

4

How we may know what influence our own prayers have had in bringing events to pass

How may we know what effect our own contribution has made when we have joined with others in prayer? Satan is apt to object that, although the prayer was answered, it was not due to any contribution from ourselves. The answers are:

1. If you wholeheartedly joined with others in praying, then it is certain that your voice helped to make it effectual. Jesus said, 'If two of you agree on earth about anything they ask, it will be done for them by my Father in heaven' (Matt. 18:19). The word 'agree' here has the meaning of harmoniously playing the same tune. Prayers are music in God's ears. The meaning is that it is not simply being of the same mind about the thing that is prayed for that is important; the emotions are also involved. It is the emotions that make the ensemble and the melody. Now if the same holy emotions are aroused by God's Spirit in your heart as in others, then you help to make up the ensemble. Indeed, without your voice, the melody would be incomplete. Especially is this so when, without your knowing, others were praying for the same thing. Then surely your prayers have had an effect as well as those of others.

2. God often provides evidence in several ways that a person's prayers have contributed to the fulfilment of something.

(a) God may so order it that a person who has prayed most for a matter has the first news of its fulfilment. Simeon had surely been most earnest in asking the Lord to send the Messiah into the world and to restore His people Israel. God had revealed to him that he should not die until he had seen the Christ for himself. So, to give Simeon evidence of God's regard for his prayers, God brought the old man into the temple at exactly the same time as the child was brought to be presented to the Lord (Luke 2:27-28). Anna, who had served God with fastings and prayers night and day, also came into the temple at exactly the same time (Luke 2:36-38). By some such circumstances or other God often witnesses to our hearts that He has heard our prayers along with those of other people.

(b) God may fill the heart with much joy in the fulfilment of what has been prayed for. This is a powerful evidence that our prayers, as well as those of others, moved the Lord to bring the matter to pass. Simeon was so overjoyed that he was even willing to die when he saw the answer to his prayers. If you have a thankful heart for a blessing received by someone for whom you joined with others in prayer, it is a sign that your prayers contributed to the result.

(c) God may stir you up to pray for yourself and incline others to do the same for you. If these prayers are heard then God most certainly had regard to your own prayers, even more than to the prayers of others who prayed for you.

5

How God helps us in our praying

When God wants us to pray He creates a praying frame of mind. He creates motives, and suggests arguments and pleas to bring before God. Along with this, we find a warming of our hearts, a lingering, a longing, and a restlessness of spirit to be alone and to pour out the soul before God. We must take careful note of such times and not neglect them, for it is certain that we then have God's ear. It is a special opportunity for prayer, such as we may never have again. The psalmist says, 'O Lord, you hear the desire of the afflicted; you will strengthen their heart; you will incline your ear' (Ps. 10:17). It is a great sign that God means to hear you when He stirs up your petitions in this way.

We should, however, note the difference between God's work and Satan's in this respect. Satan will often make unreasonable suggestions and urgings to pray, such as when we are working, or need to eat or sleep. He especially uses this device to tire out new converts. The difference is that the devil comes in a violent and imperious manner upon the conscience, but does not in the slightest way prepare the heart to pray. On the other hand, if God calls us to prayer at such extraordinary times, He fits and prepares the heart for it. He fills the soul with holy desires and gives the ability to do the thing He calls for. When God will have any great matters done, He sets His people's hearts to work at prayer by a kind of gracious instinct. He stirs them up and moves their hearts by the influence of His Holy Spirit. When Daniel knew from the Scriptures that the time of Judah's captivity was drawing to an end, he was stirred up to seek God for it (Dan. 9:2). This was just what God had said would happen. Through Jeremiah, God said that He would bring about the return of His people to their own land. 'When seventy years are completed for Babylon, I will visit you, and I will fulfil to you my promise and bring you back to this place … Then you will call upon me and come and pray to me, and I will hear you. You will seek me and find me. When you seek me with all your heart, I will be found by you, declares the LORD' (Jer. 29:10-14). We ought therefore to take careful note of the times when God especially moves our hearts to pray.

Sometimes we may have no thoughts of praying for any particular thing, but God stirs us up to pray, drawing us into His presence and moving us to call upon Him. When God thus calls us to prayer it is a sure sign that He intends to hear us.

There are also other ways in which we may be sure God will hear us.

1. When God quiets, calms and contents the heart in prayer, this is a good sign. Paul prayed earnestly for God to take away the thorn in his flesh. He said he pleaded with the Lord three times for it. God, however, assured Paul that His grace was sufficient for Him and that His power was made perfect in weakness. This calmed the mind of the apostle (2 Cor. 12:7-9). You may have been praying for a long time for God to relieve some distress, and God

comforts you with a promise like this, 'I will never leave you nor forsake you'. This quiets and contents the mind. This is God's answer, and you must take note of such answers, for they are precious.

2. When God draws near and reveals His love to you in prayer it is a token that He hears you regarding that particular request. You must take special note of this, for God, in smiling upon you and welcoming you, indicates not only that He hears your prayer, but that He accepts your person. Isaiah says, 'You shall call, and the LORD will answer; you shall cry, and he will say, Here I am' (Isa. 58:9). There may be times when you will no sooner come into God's presence to enquire of Him, but he says, 'Here I am'. When God draws near in this way it is a sure sign that He hears you.

    Daniel had fasted and prayed for three weeks, when a heavenly messenger came and told him he was highly esteemed and that his words were heard from the very first day (Dan. 10:11-12). Similarly, when God by His Spirit comes down, meets you and tells you secretly that you are His beloved and He is yours, then your prayers are certainly heard. If He accepts you as a person, how much more does He accept your prayers.

    A word of caution is needed, however. This is not always an infallible sign that a particular request will be granted, although the prayer is accepted. It is certainly an evidence that your prayer is heard. Even what you ask is agreeable to God's will and He greatly approves of you and of your request. If God then so draws near, why does He not mean to grant the request? The answer is that God approves of many things that He does not decree. God has an approving will and a decretive will. God may show His approving will of the thing you ask by drawing near in the way described. Let us suppose that you have been asking for something which is of great importance to the Church. God shows His approval for your encouragement, yet it does not necessarily follow that He has decreed to do that particular thing. His revealing of Himself is often the only answer He intended to such a prayer. It is answer enough to enjoy the assurance of God's love.

You may have prayed against some evil which you see coming upon the Church. God may still intend to bring that evil, but because He set your heart to pray against it, thereby demonstrating your own sincerity, He draws near. He tells you that it shall go well with you and that you are greatly beloved by Him. Sometimes this is the only answer God intends to give. Sometimes He does this to content the heart and prepare it for a denial. Otherwise, the denial of what you had been earnest about might cause you to question or doubt God's love.

3. It is a good sign when God stirs up a particular confidence about something, upholding us to wait for it in spite of all discouragements. This he did for David in Psalm 27. David was then in great danger from Saul or Absalom, and so frequently that to all outward probability he was never likely to live quietly at home again. David, however, prayed about this and made it the grand request of his whole life. He said. 'One thing have I asked of the LORD, that will I seek after: that I may dwell in the house of the LORD all the days of my life' (Ps. 27:4). God granted him a special faith that it would be so, for he had said previously, in verse 3: 'Though an army encamp against me, my heart

shall not fear; though war arise against me, yet I will be confident'. David's faith was vindicated. By means of prayer our hearts may be particularly strengthened and assured that God will certainly act. This is rare and extraordinary, but by no means unknown.

A caution is also required here. The thing prayed for does not always come to pass. Those persuasions stirred up by God may be, and often are, conditional upon obedience. In the case of Eli's family, God said, 'I promised that your house and the house of your father should go in and out before me [i.e. serve as priests] for ever'. But God went on to say, 'Far be it from me, for those who honour me I will honour, and those who despise me shall be lightly esteemed' (1 Sam. 2:30). Eli's sons had broken the condition which was implied in the promise and so they forfeited the blessings.

4. It is also a good sign when God creates a restless persistence in spite of all discouragements. As above, when David said, 'One thing have I asked … that will I seek after', he did not stop seeking God for it. Jesus taught the same truth in the parable of the persistent widow (Luke 18:1-8). Note, however, that it is possible to be persistent out of an unseemly desire. It is possible to ask with wrong motives, and then we shall not get what we ask (James 4:3). However, if our persistence is joined to a submisson to God's will, then it is God who has stirred it up and we may confidently expect an answer.

6

The importance of the state of our hearts after prayer

You must make sure that you have an obedient and dependent heart. If God keeps you in a more obedient frame of spirit after praying it is a sign that He intends to answer you. By contrast, David said, 'If I had cherished iniquity in my heart, the Lord would not have listened. But truly God has …attended to the voice of my prayer' (Ps. 66:18-19). That consideration acted as a curb upon David so that he was careful not to sin. If we are careless about the way we view sin, this provokes God and we shall lose whatever we might otherwise have gained by praying.

On another occasion, in Psalm 143, when David was in danger of losing his life, he especially prayed that God would direct him and keep him. David knew that, if he sinned, all his prayers would be spoilt. So, after praying that God would rescue him from his enemies, he prayed, 'Teach me to do your will, for you are my God! Let your good Spirit lead me on level ground!' (Ps. 143:10). This was more important to him than his deliverance. When God meant to give David the kingdom, God kept him innocent and his heart tender (see 1 Sam. 24:1-7).

You must continue to hope in God and wait for the fulfilment of your requests, telling the Lord that you are waiting for and expecting an answer. This is a sign that the answer is on the way. David said, 'I believe that I shall look upon the goodness of the Lord in the land of the living! Wait for the Lord; be strong, and let your heart take courage; wait for the Lord!' (Ps. 27:13-14). The hope and expectation of a godly man would make him ashamed if they were not fulfilled. Answers are therefore sure to come, and are implied by these words: 'Wait for the Lord and keep his way, and he will exalt you...' (Ps. 37:34).

7

How we may know whether the fulfilment of a matter was due to prayer or to common providence

We are prone to look upon what are truly answers to prayer as the mere outworkings of common providence. How can we discern true answers to prayer?

1. When God does something in answer to prayer He often does it in such a manner that it is unmistakable. When God hears prayers that have been a long while in the making, He usually shows half a miracle one way or the other. God shows His hand in answers to prayer in many ways. Many obstacles and difficulties may lie in the way of an answer. If they are removed, God making a key on purpose (as it were) to unlock the door, it is a sign that this is the result of prayer. There are many examples of this in the Bible: David's coming to the kingdom; Joseph's being brought out of prison; Mordecai's being exalted to honour; Peter's being released from prison. The last is a most remarkable case. Peter was sleeping between two soldiers. If they had woken up, he would have been discovered. He was in chains, but they fell off. There were guards at the door, but they took no notice. An iron gate flew open of its own accord.

2. When God uses a combination of factors like these to bring an event to pass, the lack of any one of which would have made it impossible, then it is prayer that has done it. When God delivered the people of Israel from Egypt, their captors came themselves at midnight and begged them to go, even encouraging them with gifts of jewellery. Pharaoh himself dismissed them courteously and fairly, desiring their prayers that God would bless him also. Not a dog moved its tongue, so that not even those brute creatures disturbed Israel during the night, when they would usually have been most troublesome.

3. When God brings about a sudden and unexpected accomplishment of something that has been long prayed for, perhaps even before we are aware of it, it is obviously an answer to prayer. In the previous examples, Peter was asleep and was not even dreaming of a deliverance. In Joseph's release from prison and his advancement to be the greatest in the kingdom, the suddenness of it all showed that God had remembered him and had answered his prayers.

4. When God grants more than we asked for, this is also a sign that He has heard our prayers. Paul said that God 'is able to do far more abundantly than all that we ask or think' (Eph. 3:20). Solomon asked for wisdom, but God gave him more than he asked for: peace, riches, and honour, as well as wisdom (1 Kings 3:12-13). Hannah asked for one son only, but God gave her three sons and two daughters (1 Sam. 1:11 and 2:21). When prayers are answered, blessings usually come densely packed; they

come tumbling in. The thing prayed for does not come alone.

5. When something is granted by prayer, there is often some particular circumstance or providence along with it which is a token for good, and is a seal that it is from God. When prayer had been made for a wife for Isaac, God gave a remarkable sign that the prayers had been heard. Abraham's servant had prayed in particular that the young woman who arrived to draw water and who, in response to his request, offered drink not only to him but to his camels also, would be the one God had appointed for Isaac. And Rebekah, being the first to arrive, spoke those selfsame words (Gen. 24:12-19). This was a clear indication of God's hand in the matter and so the servant bowed down and worshipped the Lord (verse 26).

Again, a consideration of the timing of the granting of our requests may help much to discern whether they are answers to prayer. God shows His wisdom and love as much in the timing as in the giving of the thing itself. God said through Isaiah, 'In a time of favour I have answered you' (Isa. 49:8). David said that he prayed to the Lord at an 'acceptable time' (Ps. 69:13). God answers in the best and most suitable time for us. He longs to be gracious, for He is a God of justice (Isa. 30:18). He is a wise God and knows the fittest times and seasons in which to show kindness and dispense His favours. Sometimes the matter is accomplished at about the same time in which we are most urgent in prayer. God said through Isaiah, 'Before they call I will answer; while they are yet speaking I will hear' (Isa. 65:24). When Peter was in prison, he came and knocked at the door at the precise moment when the Church was gathered together to pray for him (Acts 12:5-16). When Jesus healed the royal official's son, the man found that it was precisely when Jesus said to him, 'Your son will live', that he got better (John 4:46-54).

In answering prayer, God aims especially at two things. Firstly, God wishes to show His mercy so that we might be humbly grateful for His undeserved kindness to us. Secondly, God wishes to have our hearts satisfied and full of joy and contentment with the answer, so that we may delight in God's goodness. For these two purposes, He brings together the times when we have most need with those when we are most receptive to Him and our sinful desires are subdued. We are then most fit to relish God's goodness alone and not liable to be drawn away with the sensual appeal of the thing prayed for. Suppose you have prayed for a long time for assurance of salvation and joy in the Holy Spirit. When you have most need of it, (perhaps when you have seen great trouble approaching), then God has answered. This was the fittest time for God to have heard your prayer.

In the previous example of Peter, it is clear that he had been in prison for some time. God could have delivered him at any time in answer to the prayers of the Church. But God kept Peter in prison until that very night before the morning when Herod meant to bring Peter out for execution. That was the fittest time for God to answer. If what you have prayed for comes to pass when you have abandoned all other considerations and have cast yourself upon God alone, then that was the fittest time for God to act.

There is another way you may know whether a matter is granted in answer to prayer. God may deal with you in proportion to your dependence upon Him and according to the closeness of your walk with Him. David said, 'With the merciful you show yourself merciful; with the blameless man you show yourself blameless; with the purified you show yourself pure; and with the crooked you make yourself seem tortuous' (Ps. 18:25-26). When Moses' hands were down, the Amalekites were winning; but when his hands were lifted up, the Israelites were winning (Exod.17:11). It is possible to start praying earnestly for something, only to dash all prospects of an answer by falling into some sin. God would have us observe that there is a connection between our attitude towards Him and answers to prayer.

8

Observations on the effect that answers to prayers have on our hearts

If the thing granted draws your heart nearer to God then it is certain that it was granted in answer to prayer. Things obtained by prayer are made holy to us. In that way, they will not ensnare or entangle our hearts. We should return to God anything obtained by prayer and use it for God's glory. Having obtained Samuel by prayer, Hannah dedicated him to God (1 Sam. 1:27-28). Prayers answered will produce thankfulness. If the Holy Spirit stirs you up to thankfulness it is a sure sign that He was the author of your prayer. Prayer and thanks are like the double movement of the lungs; the air that is sucked in by prayer is breathed out by thanks.

Again, if the blessings obtained encourage you to go to God another time and to pray more confidently and fervently, it is a sign that you received the former by prayer. The psalmist said, 'I love the LORD, because he has heard my voice and my pleas for mercy. Because he inclined his ear to me, therefore I will call on him as long as I live' (Ps. 116:1-2).

Again, if you are stirred up to pay vows that were made as you were asking God for a particular blessing, you preserve the memory of the receipt of that blessing. It is an evidence that the blessing was obtained by prayer if God stirs you up to perform those vows.

If you can see by faith that God's hand was in the accomplishment of the matter rather than second causes, and can acknowledge that to His glory, this is because He has heard your prayers. God's intention in hearing prayer is that we might glorify Him.

Then again, if with the blessing there comes an assurance of God's love and an evidence of His favour, you will then know well enough that it was the result of prayer.

Lastly, the proof will be in the event itself. Things obtained by prayer have few thorns in them; the curse is taken out. On the other hand, what comes by ordinary providences may come with many troubles. The reason is that what comes by prayer comes as a blessing, and so no trouble is added to it (Prov. 10:22). Prayer also kills those excessive desires which cause so much vanity and vexation in our enjoyments. Things deferred but at last obtained by prayer prove most enjoyable and comforting.

9

How to remain quiet and discern an answer to prayer when what has been prayed for is not granted

This is a difficult matter. How shall we know that God has heard prayer if the thing itself is not granted? This is often the case. Christ prayed that, if it were possible, the cup might pass from Him, yet we know that it was not the Father's will that it should (Matt. 26:39,42). How do we reconcile this with the teaching in Romans 8:26 that the Holy Spirit intercedes for us when we do not know what we ought to pray? If the Holy Spirit knows that God will not grant our request, why would He stir us up to pray? You would think that the Spirit, who knows the mind of God, would always guide our hearts aright and not let us err or miss in the things we pray for. The answer is, firstly, that the Holy Spirit does not produce prayers in us according to what God's secret will and foreknowledge is, but according to what God's revealed will is. God's revealed will is presented to us both in His Word and in His providence. God leads us to pray, not always according to His secret will, but according to what is our duty to pray for most. This is similar to God's method in using preaching. God knows whom He means to convert, yet He often assists preachers to preach as much to those He does not intend to convert as to those He does mean to convert. God deals with us in these things according to what our duty is and not according to what is His decree.

Secondly, in Romans 8:26 it is said that the Spirit helps us in our weakness. He does not help us according to His vast knowledge, but helps our infirm, weak and narrow understanding. In this way He stirs up in us such things as, according to our knowledge, we have a duty to seek from God. These will be things that we consider to be most for our good and for God's glory. God accepts such desires yet does for us according to the largeness of His own love. How, then, do we deal with the problem of seemingly unanswered prayer?

The first thing is our attitude in prayer. Did we pray for something absolutely and assertively simply because we regarded it as best for ourselves? If so, we must not be surprised if the prayer is denied. We abused our privilege. But if we prayed conditionally, and with an 'if', as Christ did, and with a 'not my will, but yours be done', we are to rest in God's judgement as to what is best for us. We can then interpret the prayer as answered in spite of the denial.

We should also understand that sometimes the denial of a godly person's prayer is for his greater good and is laid as a foundation for a greater blessing. Sometimes the very denial may break your heart and bring you nearer to God. You will then begin to search your ways to see if there is something wrong with your prayers or with your general attitude. This in itself can be a great blessing. If by the loss of one thing we learn how to pray better we may be able to obtain a hundred better things afterwards. Christ prayed that the cup might pass (Matt. 26:39,42). It did not pass, but that denial was the foundation of our salvation and the way to Christ's glory.

We should also be aware of the possibility that there may be a turning of the thing desired into some other greater blessing of the same kind. All God's ways are mercy and truth to His people. God improves, collects and lays out the precious stocks of their prayers to the best advantage. God has an eye to where the greatest returns and gains may accrue. Jacob did not lay his hands of blessing as Joseph intended but crossed his hands and so blessed the younger son rather than the elder (Gen. 48:17-19). Similarly, the blessing that Isaac intended for Esau was transferred to Jacob. It was not lost (Gen. 27). There can be transfers of this sort which are not to be seen as denials but as true answers to prayer.

Again, our prayers may be answered according to their main thrust even though the actual things asked for are not received. God answers according to the hinge upon which prayer turns. We may perceive something which we feel would be much for God's glory, the good of the Church and our own comfort and happiness. God may not grant that request specifically, but because His glory was uppermost in our desires, that prayer will most certainly be answered, although in some other way. David had a great desire to build a house for the Lord, and the Lord commended him because it was in His heart to do such a thing. Nevertheless, God did not permit David himself to build the temple; that honour was given to David's son, Solomon (1 Kings 8:17-18). Sometimes, although God denies a request, He may lean a considerable way towards it in order to give satisfaction to His child. Abraham prayed earnestly for Ishmael and God went as far in granting his request as possible. God said He had heard, had blessed Ishmael, would make him fruitful and greatly increase his numbers. He would be the father of twelve rulers and God would make him into a great nation. Nevertheless, Isaac was the son with whom God would establish his covenant (Gen. 17). If God changes our requests in this way, we may be sure that there is some great

47

purpose in it and that our prayer has been the source of the miracle to bring it about.

Lastly, you must observe the effects that denials have upon your spirit. Denials may cause you to acknowledge that God is holy and righteous in His dealings with you and that your own unworthiness is the cause of His denial. God may fill your heart with a holy contentment in the denial. When Paul prayed that the thorn in the flesh might be removed, God's answer was that His grace was sufficient for Paul. This made Paul content (2 Cor. 12:9). You may still be thankful to God by trusting that whatever He has ordered for you is best, even though to your mind what has been denied would have been better. You are content with God's judgement in the matter. It is good if you can continue in prayer even when denied what you ask for. Fear the most when blessings are granted and love the most when they are denied! The Psalmist complained to God 'How long will you be angry with your people's prayers?' (Ps. 80:4). But he would not give up praying, even though God did not seem to hear. So you must pray on, even though you do not have an answer in this life. Fair-minded people are moved by those who take rebuffs and denials well, for they know that proud people will not do this. God, also, is moved by such a humble attitude in His children.

10

A reproof for those who will not look for blessings from their prayers

Some people offer prayers and are earnest in begging things from God, but they do not pay any more regard to their prayers afterwards than if they had not prayed at all. They may have a great stock of prayers but they make no attempt to calculate what profits they have gained by praying. Instead, they become discouraged and doubt whether they will ever hear of their prayers again. They might as well have been speaking mere words into the air. Such people despise God's gracious provision for them, not knowing the power of prayer. They also despise the Lord Himself. Not to answer when a question is put to you, is contempt; and not to take any notice when an answer is given is no less contemptuous. Suppose you had written a letter to a close friend about an important business and had urgently requested an answer. If you totally ignored his reply would you not be guilty of contempt? Or if you should not bother to read his answer when he wrote, would he not have cause to be angry with you? So here, when you have earnestly sought God over something and you take no notice of His answer you will be in contempt of God. This is a common fault among believers. You may not stop praying but you do not expect answers as you should. Let us look at the reasons for this.

1. The first is lack of assurance. Because you have a weak assurance that God accepts you as you are, your confidence that He will hear your prayers is also weak. God does first of all accept us as we are and this gives us confidence that He will also accept our prayers. As we saw in chapter 1, this truth is found in 1 John 5:13-15: 'I write these things to you who believe in the name of the Son of God that you may know that you have eternal life. And this is the confidence that we have towards him, that if we ask anything according to his will he hears us. And if we know that he hears us in whatever we ask, we know that we have the requests that we have asked of him.'

   Notice how John links three things together as effects and consequences of each other. Firstly, he wants his readers to know that they may be assured that eternal life and heaven are theirs. Following from that will spring a confidence that God will hear them. God will have His ears open to them and His heart will be warm with love for them. Then thirdly, if they are confident that God hears them it will follow that they will have an assurance that God will grant them anything they desire that is according to His will. When we are assured that God has given us His Son we will then easily believe and expect that God will give us everything else that we need (Rom. 8:32).

   When we have grasped the fact that God is our Father we shall then easily understand the words of Jesus in Matthew 7:11: 'If you then, who are evil, know how to give good gifts to your children, how much more will your Father who is in heaven give good gifts to those who ask him!' If God gave you His Son when you did not pray to Him, how much more will He give you the things you do pray for!

2. You may feel discouraged because your prayers are weak. You may believe that God accepts you as you are and yet complain that, because your prayers are poor and weak, God will not take any notice of them. We may answer this in four ways.

(a) Firstly, do you pray with all your might? Then even though that 'might' may be weak in itself, yet because it is all the might you have, it will be accepted. God accepts according to what we have, and not according to what we do not have (2 Cor. 8:12).

(b) You must remember that God does not hear you for the sake of your prayers (though not without them), but for His name's sake, for His Son's sake, and because you are His child. When a child cries, the weaker it is, the more a mother is concerned about it.

(c) Prayer may be weak as a performance, yet it may still be strong enough. Even a weak prayer can set our strong God to work. Prayer does not succeed because of the performance itself, but because of the name in which it is offered – even Christ's. Faith attributes all to God, and so does prayer. As faith is merely a receiving grace, so prayer is a begging grace. God fully accepts even the weakest act of faith. Prayer is the means God has provided to convey His blessings, and so it does not matter whether it is weak or strong in our estimation of it.

(d) You must not judge your prayers by their eloquence or by the stirrings of heart you have when offering them. The strength and vigour of prayer is to be estimated from the faith, sincerity and obedience expressed in it. It is not the volume of the preacher's voice that moves an intelligent hearer, but the weight and holiness of the matter and the spirit of the preacher. It is not gifts, but graces, that move the Lord in prayer. The strength of prayer does not lie in words, but in the fact that it has the power to influence God. Prayers do not move God as an orator moves His hearers, but as a child moves His father. God is more concerned about the spirit in which we pray than in our choice of words.

3. A third discouragement is the failure to receive answers. You may have prayed often and long and yet your prayers have seldom or never been answered. You therefore have little confidence that your prayers have ever been heard. Others have dividends from their prayers but you seem to get nothing. To deal with this problem note:

   (a) You have the more reason to wait, for you may have the more answers to come. As wicked people treasure up wrath, so godly people store up mercy, and especially by their prayers. Answers and blessings often come thick together.

   (b) Even if you seem to have few answers, yet your reward is with the Lord. Praying is like preaching. A man may preach faithfully for many years and yet see no conversions. He must not give up but remind himself after every sermon that every worker will receive his reward according to his own labour (1 Cor. 3:8). This reward does not depend on the success or otherwise of his preaching. When you pray, although you seem to miss again and again, you must not be discouraged because your reward is with the Lord and will be received one day.

(c) God may delay His answers, not because He does not hear you, but to test you. He may be testing your faithfulness in some duty.

(d) God may delay so long that you have given up expecting His answer. The elect cry day and night (Luke 18:7-8), but God waits for such a long time that, when He does come, He does not find faith. His people have given up expecting and they have forgotten their prayers. It is then that God does things that they do not look for, for His own glory's sake.

4. There are other discouragements for which we ourselves are to blame. I will list three:

(a) Slothfulness in prayer. If we are not earnest and fervent in prayer, how can we expect God to give us anything good? Jacob obtained what he needed by praying and wrestling (Gen. 32:24-32). Christ said that many will try to enter the kingdom of God, but you must make every effort to do so (Luke 13:24). When we know these things and yet are slothful, how can we expect any answers at all? God will behave as though He were asleep. Those prayers that awaken God must first awaken us. Those prayers that stir God must first stir us to lay hold of God. As obedience strengthens faith and assurance, so fervency in prayer brings about the confidence of being heard. In all things, slothfulness discourages and weakens expectation. Does anyone expect that riches will come when he does his business negligently? You cannot expect an answer if you are slothful in prayer.

(b) Another cause of sinful discouragement is if you look at prayer only as a duty to be performed rather than as a means of obtaining blessings. Think of a doctor who

53

has a sick employee and who prescribes a medicine for him, ordering him to take it. If the employee takes the medicine only as a matter of duty to please the doctor, but not in any way as a means of curing his illness, what sort of attitude is that? Most people seem to use prayer like that. They take prayer as a prescription only, but not as a means of blessing. They come to God daily, but only as to an employer by way of duty. They do not come to God as to a Father, and so it is small wonder if they have little expectation from their prayers. You should look for two things in prayer. Firstly, prayer is a command from God. Secondly, prayer is a means of receiving promised blessings. Prayer is firstly an act of obedience and secondly it is an act of faith in God's promises. When you ask you must believe and not doubt (James 1:6). Most people seem to perform prayer only as an act of obedience, but if you pray in faith, looking to God's promises, you may expect God to answer you.

(c) A third sinful discouragement is to return to sin after praying. If you have prayed for some blessing and are full of confidence that your prayers are heard, yet fall into sin, that sin will dash all your hopes. You will feel that you have wrecked your prayers and that they will not reach heaven. Sin may indeed hinder the obtaining of your petitions; but it is not so much past sins that are a hindrance. It is more likely to be your present unhelpful attitude towards God which hinders your sense of blessing through prayer.

Part Two

God speaking peace

*'Let me hear what God the L*ORD
will speak,
For he will speak peace to his people,
his saints'

11

God promises peace to distressed consciences

I have dealt with the main point of my text. But there is much more in this verse. I shall consider it more briefly.

This psalm was originally written to prophesy of, and pray for, the return of God's people from captivity in Babylon. However, it looks beyond that to the peace and glory brought by Christ. So 'peace' does not just mean outward prosperity. It refers to speaking peace to distressed consciences. Isaiah promised such peace (see Isa. 48:20-22; 57:14-21). Many people had mourned the loss of the temple worship and thought that God intended to destroy them. As these texts from Isaiah show, these people were refreshed by inward peace as well as outward restoration. So this is the kind of peace I shall consider in looking at how God deals with His people.

God does not always give peace to His people immediately
The first thing to notice is that God does not always give peace to His children. The text says, 'He will speak peace'. That suggests that at that time God was not giving peace – rather the opposite. For examples of this, look at passages like Isaiah 63:10; Jeremiah 31:20; Psalm 50:7; 51:8; Job 13:24-26.

God does not interrupt the peace of His people without good reason. Often it is because they have fallen into some gross folly. The fact that God says 'but let them not turn back to folly' indicates that it was their foolishness which had caused God to be angry with them. That is where all the quarrels that God has against people begin (Isa. 63:8; 57:17). This anger springs from love.

We should learn three lessons from this.

1. If you value peace with God, beware of turning to folly. If we fight against our sins, God will be at peace with us; but if we make peace with our sins, God will be at war with us.

2. If God has a quarrel with you, seek to be reconciled to Him. Paul says, 'Do not let the sun go down on your anger' (Eph. 4:26): reconcile yourself to your offended brother before night falls. In the same way, do not let the sun go down on God's anger: make and renew your peace with God before you sleep. Then, as David says, you may lie down and sleep in peace (Ps. 4:8).

3. If the peace of God's own people may be often interrupted, what wrath is reserved for those who are open rebels? '"There is no peace", says my God, "for the wicked"' (Isa. 57:21). Think about that, if you are determined to go on in sin.

Only God can give peace to His people

Only God can give peace to His people. Nothing else can help in times of distress. Why is this?

1. God is the sovereign Lord of all the world. Proclaiming war and peace with foreign states is the prerogative of earthly kings. So it is with God, who is the King of kings.

2. God is the Judge of all the world. When a man stands trial, it does not matter how many people tell him that his cause will go well. Only the judge can acquit him. So it is with God. The only way to be at peace is to make peace with God.

3. Peace of conscience must be created: it does not come naturally to us. God must speak a word of power, or our hearts will be full of turmoil, like the raging sea which cannot rest (Isa. 57:20).

4. Only God can cure the wounds of conscience in His people. The main thing that hurts them is the loss of God's favour. So nothing can give them peace except for the restoring of His favour. When a child is crying for its mother, nobody else can quieten it. So it is with a poor soul who cries for God day and night.

So if you are in distress of spirit, lacking peace of conscience, wait upon God. Use the means He has appointed.

Are you troubled by hellish blasphemies coming into your thoughts? Only God can speak peace and rebuke Satan for you. He can do it as easily as he rebuked Laban and prevented him attacking Jacob (Gen. 31:24). So wait upon God and look up to Him.

When you come to die, you want to die in peace. At death you will send for a good minister, or a good friend, to give you comfort; but if God will not speak peace to you, how can they?

People may come to you and say 'peace, peace', as they did in Jeremiah 6:14; 8:11; but listen to what God says. He alone can give real peace. Make sure of Him before you come to die. Would any wise prince defer making peace with his enemy until the battle had begun? How foolish then are those who neglect seeking God until the assault of death comes, and the king of fears has surrounded them with all His terrors?

God can easily give peace to His people

God can easily give His people peace, however great their distress. The psalmist says that God will '*speak* peace'. It is as easy for Him to give peace as it is for you to speak a word. It is a comfort to us to know that, while only God can give peace, He can easily do it.

1. When God speaks, He brings things into being with a word, as He did at first. He simply said, 'Let there be light', and there was light. In the same way, if He says, 'Let there be peace', there is peace. When the storm was at its height, and the waves most raging, yet at one word of Christ's they were all still. 'Even the the wind and the sea obey him' (Mark 4:41). In the same way, when temptations are most fierce, and your doubts most powerful, God can still them with a word.

2. The light which God gives to a man's spirit when He speaks peace is certain and infallible. No objection or temptation can darken or obscure it when it shines. No creature can separate from His love, or the assurance of it.

   It is certain because God speaks so infallibly and distinctly that the soul knows the meaning of it. When the

Holy Spirit speaks, He speaks as a witness, and therefore puts an end to a man's doubts.

It is also satisfying: it dispels darkness, answers all objections, and so gives peace. It shows the soul that God's free grace in Christ answers every argument that he or the devil can raise.

This gives comfort to people who are in distress. Sometimes people think that their case is hopeless. They are in despair. But consider how easy it is for your condition to be changed, even in a moment. One good word from God can dispel all your fears, even after twenty years of despair. God often does more in a moment than Satan can do in many years with all the objections he can muster. Sometimes, when God gives peace to someone, He gives him such satisfaction that he would be willing to have many more years of spiritual conflict just to enjoy half an hour of such light. You may think yourself far off from peace, but God can speak peace to those who are afar off as easily as to those who are near (Eph. 2:17). When He does, all your doubts and distresses will be forgotten, as a woman forgets her labour pains when her child is born (John 16:21).

This also gives comfort when the Church is in distress (as it was when the psalm was written). God can redeem His Church with a word. God said that Jerusalem would be inhabited and the towns of Judah rebuilt. He commanded the waters to dry up to allow His people to pass through. He instructed Cyrus to command that Jerusalem be rebuilt (Isa. 44:26-28). So go to God. Trust Him in all the troubles of the Church. This is what the psalmist did. He remembered what God had done in the past, and appealed to Him to act again (Ps. 44:1-4).

God will eventually give peace to His people

God will certainly give peace to His people. God may be very angry. God's people may be greatly distressed. Nevertheless, in the end God will give peace to His people. We have already seen that only God can give peace, and that He can easily do it. But how do we know that God will certainly give peace in the end?

1. Consider who this God is. He is the Lord, and therefore able to do as He pleases. More, He is 'the God of peace' (Rom. 15:33; 16:20; Phil. 4:9; 1 Thess. 5:23; Heb. 13:20), and therefore willing to give peace. When it says He is 'the God of peace', it means that He is infinitely full of peace. Thoughts of love and peace boil within Him, and must be expressed. Besides, God's Son has obtained peace for us, so God will give us peace.

2. Consider the people to whom God is to give peace. They are *God's* people, as the text says. God will not forsake His people (1 Sam. 12:22). In Jeremiah 31:20, God describes Ephraim as his darling child. Although God spoke against him, yet He says that he cannot forget his child: 'Therefore my heart yearns for him; I will surely have mercy on him, declares the Lord.'

3. If God did not eventually give peace, His people would indeed return to folly. The text indicates that God gives peace so that they do not return to folly. In Psalm 125, God says, 'the sceptre of wickedness shall not rest on the land allotted to the righteous, lest the righteous stretch out their hands to do wrong'. So that psalm ends, 'Peace be upon Israel.'

In the same way, God gives inward peace. He does not allow the rod of Satan or of His own heavy displeasure to rest on their hearts. Otherwise, they would return to the pleasures of sin; for every creature must have some delight. They would tire of doing good if God did not in the end give peace. 'I will not contend forever, nor will I always be angry; for the spirit would grow faint before me' (Isa. 57:16).

Do not presume on God's goodness. Let the fact that God will eventually give peace encourage you to return to Him. As Samuel said to the Israelites, 'Do not turn aside from following the LORD, but serve the LORD with all your heart. And do not turn aside after empty things that cannot profit or deliver, for they are empty. For the LORD will not forsake his people, for his great name's sake, because it has pleased the LORD to make you a people for himself ... Only fear the LORD and serve him faithfully with all your heart. For consider what great things he has done for you' (1 Sam. 12:20-24).

Part Three

The folly of turning back

*'Let me hear what God the L*ord
will speak,
For he will speak peace to his people,
his saints;
But let them not turn back to folly'

12

The foolishness of turning back after God has spoken peace

If God has brought peace to our hearts, it would be foolish to relapse into sin. Rather it is a time when we should be filling our minds with reasons to remain faithful. As Ezra prayed, 'You, our God, have punished us less than our iniquities deserved and have given us such a remnant as this, shall we break your commandments again? ... Would you not be angry with us until you consumed us?' (Ezra 9:13,14).

Here, then, are seven pieces of advice to store up in our hearts.

1. Turning back from God after receiving His message of peace is foolishness because it is particularly offensive to Him

It was an aggravation of Solomon's sin that God had appeared to him twice (1 Kings 11:9). We do not expect the same direct appearances that Solomon had, but Jesus has promised to be with us and reveal Himself to us by His Spirit (John 14:21). When we sin, we are despising this special love that He has shown us. As human beings, we understand how hurtful it is when we show love to someone and they despise it. It was an aggravation of Absalom's sin that he actively rebelled against his father, King David, with whom he had so recently been reconciled (see 2 Samuel chapters 14 and 15). Such behaviour, even in human relationships is hurtful and unnatural. Think how you are treating God!

2. Turning back from God is foolishness because of the harm it will do us

Quite apart from the grief it causes our loving heavenly Father, think how hurtful it is to ourselves.

(a) Our first enjoyment of God's peace came as a great relief from the burden and sorrow caused by our sin. We already know how bitter sin is and how painful it is to live with a guilty conscience. Remember how horrible that was. Do you really want to go through all that again?

(b) Think what efforts you had to go to in order to gain peace in the first place. Think of the prayers offered, the tears shed, and the resolutions you made. If you went to such trouble to get clean, why would you be so foolish as to wallow in the mud again?

3. Turning back from God is foolishness because of the good things that we will lose

Turning back to sinful ways will rob us of joy, peace and the experience of the loving kindness of God. Psalm 51 tells us how when David sinned, he lost his peace and with it the joy of salvation (see Ps. 51:12). If we were to indulge in a sin that gave us the whole world, it could not make up for the loss of one hour's true fellowship with God. God's peace 'surpasses all understanding' (Phil. 4:7) and is worth vastly more than anything sin can offer us. God's 'steadfast love is better than life' itself (Ps. 63:3), so why risk losing it even for a moment?

4. Turning back from God is foolishness because the pleasures of sin will disappoint us

The pleasures people derive from sinning are always empty and will not last, but sadly unconverted people know no better. But now that you have come to know God, those 'pleasures' will be even less satisfying.

(a) You now have a sensitive conscience that will trouble you and cause grief if you commit sin.

(b) You have a new nature that finds no pleasure in sinning so it is as if only half of you can enjoy sin in any case.

(c) The goodness of God has spoiled your appetite for sin. As Jesus said: 'No one after drinking old wine desires new, for he says, "The old is better"' (Luke 5:39). When we become Christians, we find that knowing God is like a rich feast. Sin may promise many wonderful things but we shall find it like a very poor meal in comparison.

5. When we have experienced God's peace, that is a time when we should be especially devoted to fearing Him

If we have been granted peace, we should not only be grateful for the blessing but even more for the God who has given it. This is a time to dwell not just on our duties of obedience, or our fear of judgement, but on the relationship that we have with God as His children. Take special notice of the warning not to 'grieve the Holy Spirit' who has 'sealed us for the day of redemption' (Eph. 4:30).

We recognise that God is angry with sin and with unrepentant sinners, but if you are His child, then sin affects Him even more deeply: He is grieved by it. What should He do with you in this case? If He were to afflict you with troubles to turn you away from your sin it would actually grieve Him even more. As the prophet spoke about a rebellious Israel: 'In all their affliction he was afflicted' (Isa. 63:9). Even a good human father is distressed when he finds it necessary to discipline one of his children. If you have any love for God in your heart, do not treat Him so unkindly!

6. When we have experienced God's peace, that is a time when we need to be especially careful

Times of spiritual blessing —in this case an experience of God's peace—can often be followed by dangerous temptations. It was after God had answered Hezekiah's desperate prayers and extended his life that he fell into sin (see 2 Kings 20). Peter had seen Jesus transfigured and experienced many other blessings but then fell into self-confidence (see Matt. 26:30-35). The devil is especially active when blessings have come from God to us, and we must therefore be especially watchful in case we are defeated through a false sense of security. We are in danger if we think that forgiveness can easily be obtained. When you are tempted to go back into sin, remember how hard it was for you to gain peace in the first place and how hard it was for Jesus to purchase that pardon for you by going to the cross. God does not owe you forgiveness, He has been wonderfully generous. Do not risk losing all this. 'Sin no more, that nothing worse may happen to you' (John 5:14).

7. If God has assured us of His love for us by speaking peace, this ought to restrain us from foolishly returning to sinful ways

Some have thought that being assured of forgiveness would be dangerous for us, on the grounds that it would make us casual and presumptuous about sinning but, rightly understood, the opposite is the case. When God has spoken peace to us, it is a strong motive to remain faithful and not return to foolish, sinful ways.

The first letter of John was written to help believers gain assurance (1 John 5:13), but John also says that he is writing 'so that you may not sin' (1 John 2:1). He goes on to say that 'If anyone does sin, we have an advocate with the Father' and later says that anyone who has this hope of new life in Christ and who knows 'what kind of love the Father has for us', 'purifies himself as he [God] is pure' (1 John 3:1-3).

If we only have love for ourselves then of course we will feel free to do anything that appears to serve our own interests. And if too much self-love remains in us as Christians, that may explain why God does not trust us with a firm assurance. However, if love for God has been strongly planted in our lives, that will stir us to holiness of life and hatred of sin. The love of God for us in Christ constrains us to see things in a new way and motivates us to live for Him (2 Cor. 5:14-15). If God has truly worked in our hearts, this will be the sure consequence.

13

A word to those who do fall back into the same sins

This seems an appropriate place to consider the case of a person who has experienced God's forgiveness and peace after struggling with a particular sin but then falls back into the same sin afterwards. Some have thought that this cannot happen and that we are given some special immunity to that sin once we have truly repented. Others have suggested that if we did fall into the same sin, there would be no possibility of restoration because the door of God's mercy would be closed to us. Here are some thoughts to comfort and encourage us.

1. The Bible nowhere shuts the door of mercy to those who relapse into the same sin, especially where this has happened because of a lack of understanding or by foolish impulse rather than being a deliberate act of wickedness.

2. In fact there are passages and promises specifically designed to encourage and restore those who may fear that they have sinned away any further opportunity of forgiveness. We have a good example in Hosea where the prophet is given a message to a people who had repeatedly returned to the same foolish idolatry. God says: 'I will heal their apostasy; I will love them freely' (Hosea 14:4). God is even

prepared to forgive the fact that they have abused His love for them. God's love is FREE. That thought should keep us from sinning; but when we fall it also gives us mercy and repentance.

In Isaiah 55, God speaks of His covenant mercies shown to David (v. 3) and then in verse 7 he says that He will 'abundantly pardon' (literally, 'multiply to pardon'). There is multiplied forgiveness for multiplied sin!

In Jeremiah 3, God likens His people to an unfaithful wife who has deserted her husband for a succession of lovers and yet expects to be welcomed back by her husband (vv. 1-5). The very idea appears outrageous and impossible yet, in verses 12 and 14, God still appeals to the people to return and promises mercy to them. If He can speak this way to a whole nation, surely that will also be the case for us as individuals.

3. There are also some particular examples of people who are regarded in the Bible as faithful believers despite falling repeatedly into the same sort of sin.

(a) Samson was a godly man according to Hebrews 11, but was repeatedly tempted into sin by Philistine women. In the first recorded case it was despite the advice of his parents (Judges 14:3) and it had an outcome that should surely have convinced him of his foolishness. Nevertheless, twenty years later he repeated his sin (Judges 15:20–16:1) and only narrowly escaped with his life (16:3), and then sinned again with Delilah and sank to the position of a weak, blind, prisoner (16:4-22). This should not be any encouragement to us to sin; but nevertheless God heard his final prayer and used him to win a great victory.

(b) Jehoshophat king of Judah committed a great sin by joining with wicked king Ahab of Israel (2 Chron. 18:1-3). He was warned beforehand by the prophet Micaiah about the outcome but still went ahead and nearly lost his life. Another prophet rebuked him afterwards, telling him that it is wrong to help the wicked (19:2). Yet, even after God had given him a great victory over the Moabites and Ammonites (20:1-30) he relapsed into the very same sin by making an alliance with wicked Ahaziah of Israel, another enterprise that God rebuked by the prophet Eliezer and brought to disaster (20:35-37).

(c) The apostle Peter may appear generally to be a bold believer; but on three different occasions he was overcome by fear. It was fear of the consequences that led him to urge Jesus not to go to Jerusalem to suffer (Matt. 16:21-23). Jesus had to rebuke him sharply and urge all the disciples to self-denial (v. 24). Yet, despite the wonderful confirmation of Jesus' glory that Peter witnessed when Jesus was transfigured (Matt. 17:1-8) and the loving warnings that Jesus gave (Matt. 26:31-35), he still denied knowing Jesus (Matt. 26:69-75). That failure caused Peter great sorrow but, after His resurrection, Jesus showed special love to him by making sure that he was told the good news (Mark 16:7) and by restoring him so tenderly (John 21:15-19). And although Peter afterwards became very bold in some circumstances (Acts 4:13), he was again led astray in his treatment of the Gentiles by fear of some who held wrong views about circumcision (Gal. 2:11-13). This is also an example of how the same root sin (in this case, fear) can express itself in different ways.

4. Even if there were no examples in Scripture, there are some general principles that might lead us to the same conclusion.

If we can fall into some other sin after conversion—and surely we can, and do —why should we deny the possibility that we might fall into the one particular sin that most troubled us earlier? Of course, we may have some particular aversion to it, but if it is possible to fall into one sin, it is possible to fall into any. Why should we assume that repentance carries with it some special power to make us immune from a particular temptation? There is no promise of that in the Scriptures. Certainly, we should be striving against sin and our hatred of it should be increasing, but we are not made perfect in this life and we must continue to live by faith. God has indeed promised that though a believer may fall 'he shall not be cast headlong, for the LORD upholds his hand' (Ps. 37:24); but that does not protect us from stumbling again in the future. Repentance, like prayer and listening to preaching, is used by God to help preserve us from future sin, but none of these things is an infallible protection.

5. The warnings of the Bible also imply that any sort of sin may overtake any one of us and that we therefore need to be careful. Paul tells us that when a fellow-believer falls, he should be restored in a spirit of gentleness and even the most mature believers, who are those called to this task, are warned to take care lest they themselves are also tempted (Gal. 6:1).

   We are also told that we all suffer the same sorts of temptation and therefore we all need to be on our guard. 'Therefore let anyone who thinks that he stands take heed lest he fall' (1 Cor. 10:12). In taking to heart this serious warning, bear in mind the following:

   (a) Some sins are more gross than others and bring scandal on the Church. We may expect believers to be less susceptible to some of these but more prone to things like rash anger, love of the world, and spiritual pride.

(b) Grace weakens our desires for sin but doesn't take them entirely away and therefore we have a continuing struggle. 'I have the desire to do what is right, but not the ability to carry it out', says Paul (Rom. 7:18). Even in those who are most spiritually-minded he seems to expect that 'the desires of the flesh are against the Spirit, and the desires of the Spirit are against the flesh' (Gal. 5:17).

(c) It is, of course, a serious matter to fall into sin; and all the more so if we repeat the same sin. It will cause us great grief if we are spiritually-minded and is an aggravated offence against God, as we see for example in the sad cry, 'How often they rebelled against him in the wilderness' (Ps. 78:40).

(d) We would be in a very dangerous position indeed if we were repeatedly returning to the same sin.

(e) We cannot strictly calculate how often a person may fall into sin, repent and be forgiven; but it is helpful to consider that (i) there are degrees of repentance. No repentance is ever perfect but some may be more thorough and life-changing than others and some people will make better progress than others. (ii) God deals with us in different ways. Sometimes it is gradual, as with the sun in winter which may thaw the ice a little during the day while at night it freezes again and so the process is repeated the next day with apparently little effect. But then, there comes a more general thaw as the seasons progress and the sun gets stronger. It may take a time, therefore, before the love of God, as it were, thaws our hearts and drives out all the sinful indifference.

However, we must be very careful that we are not hardened by the deceitfulness of sin. God will not always strive with us and if we are His children and we are not responding to His gentle promptings (like the thawing ice), He may send us a great trouble to drive us away from our sin.

If these encouragements from God are making you less sensitive to sin and you are taking His forgiveness for granted, then your case is dangerous and may prove desperate. But if you find that you are struggling with your sin, that you want to overcome and that you are afraid of falling back into sin, then you may be sure that God's love will triumph in the end.

Final appeals

If it is foolish to go back to the same sin, even if we do repent and are forgiven, how much more foolish it is to fall away entirely! How sad is the case of those who try a little religion, show some interest, but then go back to their sinful ways! Alas, poor souls, where will you go? Will you find such a God elsewhere? As Peter said to Jesus: 'You have the words of eternal life' (John 6:68). Can the world give you the peace that only Jesus offers? Is the devil really able to make up for what you are losing? You are bringing dishonour on God if you return to sin and you are returning to folly. If you think that the unbelieving world will think well of you, you will be disappointed. The backslider is like salt that has lost its taste which 'is no longer good for anything except to be thrown out and trampled under people's feet' (Matt. 5:13). Oh return, while you still have the opportunity!

And you who do enjoy peace and communion with God, take good care not to lose it, because you will never have such a God again.

Grace
Publications

Grace Publications Trust

Grace Publications Trust is a not-for-profit organisation that exists to glorify God by making the truth of God's Word (as declared in the Baptist Confessions of 1689 and 1966) clear and understandable, so that:

- Christians will be helped to preach Christ
- Christians will know Christ better and delight in Him more
- Christians will be equipped to live for Christ
- Seekers will come to know Christ

From its beginning in the late 1970s the Trust has published simplified and modernised versions of important Christian books written earlier, for example by some of the Reformers and Puritans. These books have helped introduce the riches of the past to a new generation and have proved particularly useful in parts of Asia and Africa where English is widely spoken as a second language. These books are now appearing in editions co-published with Christian Focus as *Grace Essentials*.

More details of the Trust's work can be found on the web site at *www.gracepublications.co.uk*.

Christian Focus Publications

Our mission statement –

STAYING FAITHFUL

In dependence upon God we seek to impact the world through literature faithful to His infallible Word, the Bible. Our aim is to ensure that the Lord Jesus Christ is presented as the only hope to obtain forgiveness of sin, live a useful life and look forward to heaven with Him.

Our Books are published in four imprints:

CHRISTIAN
FOCUS

popular works including biographies, commentaries, basic doctrine and Christian living.

CHRISTIAN
HERITAGE

books representing some of the best material from the rich heritage of the church.

MENTOR

books written at a level suitable for Bible College and seminary students, pastors, and other serious readers. The imprint includes commentaries, doctrinal studies, examination of current issues and church history.

CF4·K

children's books for quality Bible teaching and for all age groups: Sunday school curriculum, puzzle and activity books; personal and family devotional titles, biographies and inspirational stories – because you are never too young to know Jesus!

Christian Focus Publications Ltd,
Geanies House, Fearn, Ross-shire,
IV20 1TW, Scotland, United Kingdom.
www.christianfocus.com